Lost Love

BY KENNETH BRUCE WELCKLE

DORRANCE
PUBLISHING CO
EST. 1920
PITTSBURGH, PENNSYLVANIA 15238

Dorrance Publishing Co
585 Alpha Drive
Suite 103
Pittsburgh, PA 15238
Visit our website at *www.dorrancebookstore.com*

ISBN: 978-1-6366-1377-2
eISBN: 978-1-6366-1954-5

"They will never be your lost love."

—KENNETH BRUCE
WELCKLE

CAST OF CHARACTERS

REBECCA: Early 30s, athletic and keeps herself in shape. Has blonde hair. Always has a smile on her face. Also was a cheerleader in high school. She also likes to wear women's fedora hats as well.

KAREN: In her early 40s with red hair and body type average. Somebody who has good wit. Is a good friend of Rebecca.

JOHN: A guy in his early 30s, body type average. Wears glasses and has black hair. Somebody who is interested in history as well. Type of guy who can get along with anybody and has a good sense of humor. Always is a gentleman.

BAKERY OWNER KEITH: A veteran who served in the U.S. Military. Owns the local bakery in Mankato. Highly respected member in the community. Somebody who always seems to have good advice to give, and also a lover of Shakespeare as well.

JOHN'S FIANCÉ JILL: Dance instructor, late 30s to early 40s. Slim and slender with brunette hair. Kind and friendly.

SYNOPSIS

Rebecca is taking much needed advice from her coworker Karen at the law office firm that Rebecca works at in Minneapolis. She takes a much needed vacation from work. Heads for her hometown of Mankato. She runs unexpectedly into her former high school sweetheart, John. They spend time together, catching up with each other. Will they rekindle their love for one other, or will John forever be her lost love?

Lights up

SETTING: Law firm office in Minneapolis

TIME: Present

Law office back wall is right center, desk is center, office door is left center. A woman wearing a women's casual business suit is typing on her laptop. On the desk is a picture of her that was taken on the day of graduation from law school. The other picture is her first day at the law office. On the back wall is her law school diploma. Also on her desk are brown paper files as well.

KAREN
Rebecca, some of us are going for a drink after work.

REBECCA
Karen, thanks for the offer. But I'm currently busy.

KAREN
Rebecca, when was the last time you actually took a vacation?

REBECCA
Before I started here.

Karen

Sweet Jesus, woman, even the Queen of England takes a vacation.

Rebecca

Karen, you are probably right. I do need to take break from work. Take a vacation for myself. Just forget about work for a while.

Karen

Good. I already called a bed-and-breakfast that recently opened outside of your home of Mankato. They are expecting you tomorrow.

Rebecca arrives at the bed-and-breakfast outside of her hometown of Mankato.

As she pulls into the driveway, she sees that bed-and-breakfast has a look of a barn. Also sees the other building on the property is a cottage. That was the type of cottage that you would have found in 1780s Virginia. Also the same distance from the bed-and-breakfast as well is a small vegetable garden.

There is also a stone barn on the property as well. The barn doors are reclaimed barn wood. The upper halves of two barn doors are two round windows with white trim around them. In the middle of the property outside of the bed-and-breakfast is a round brick flowerbed with a wooden sign in the middle of it saying: "Enjoy life to the fullest or otherwise it will pass you by."

REBECCA

That's definitely a different look for a bed-and-breakfast. She parks the car and after grabbing her suitcase Rebecca enters downstage right, walks into the bed-and-breakfast. The front desk is left center. She heads for the desk and rings the bell on the desk.

REBECCA

Anybody here?

A couple of minutes later, an man comes around the corner. He is in his early 30s, with short black hair, wearing glasses. He is in a pair of blue jeans and t-shirt, and his left arm is in a sling.

JOHN

Rebecca, what are you doing here?

REBECCA

My coworker Karen at the law office told me that I needed to take a vacation. I see your business degree finally paid off. How come you decided to have your bed-and-breakfast have the look of a barn?

JOHN

I wanted my bed-and-breakfast to stand out from your typical bed-and-breakfast. I hope that this isn't awkward.

REBECCA

That was past all right.

JOHN

I can show you to the guestroom. Carry your suitcases for you.

REBECCA

That's perfectly all right.

JOHN

I will not have a guest carrying her own suitcases to her room. That would be completely un gentlemanlike.

REBECCA

You always drive a hard bargain.

JOHN

I guess I missed my calling as a salesman, then.

REBECCA

Boy, it is getting deep in here.

JOHN

Good thing I have a pair of boots by the door that we can use if need be. You can have any of the guestrooms down on the second floor of your choice.

John picks up Rebecca's suitcase with his right hand and they head up to the second floor, where the guestrooms are. Rebecca opens the guestroom door and John puts down her suitcase.

SETTING: The guestroom has a bed against one wall and a nightstand by the bed with a lamp on it in case any guests want to read a book. There is a dresser in the room. By the door is a wooden coatrack. There is a window on the wall facing the bed.

REBECCA
John, where did you get that old-fashioned antique coatrack from?

JOHN
I picked it up at an antique store a couple of days ago. Good chance of room. This is one of the most requested rooms at the bed-and-breakfast. Also that window there gives you a beautiful view of the countryside as well.

REBECCA
You can't beat seeing the view of the beautiful countryside when you are waking up in the morning.

JOHN
I won't disagree with that.

Later that evening, Rebecca is in the kitchen making herself some hot chocolate and putting some marshmallows on top of it. Then she walks outside on the porch and sits down on the porch swing. A couple of minutes later, John joins her.

REBECCA
John, your mom would make the best hot chocolate in town whenever I would come over to your house.

JOHN
You always had to have three marshmallows in yours. I suppose you haven't had an old-fashioned cooked meal in a long time.

REBECCA

True. I've forgotten how peaceful and quiet it is in the country compared to living in Minneapolis, despite all that Minneapolis has to offer. The restaurants, art galleries, and history museums, it can't beat the appeal of living in the country.

JOHN

That's something city folks will never understand, where living in the big city people don't take the time to enjoy the simple things in life.

REBECCA

You still have a way with words.

JOHN

It's one of my hidden talents.

REBECCA

You should write a book and call it "The World According to John."

JOHN

I don't know about that. Besides, do you really think that somebody would want to take advice from somebody who broke his arm doing something really stupid just a couple of days before his wedding? But that's for another time.

He gets up from the porch swing.

JOHN

I'll be heading back in. Have a good night's sleep.

REBECCA

Thanks.

The next morning in the kitchen, Rebecca comes in and sees John making breakfast.

JOHN

Good morning, there.

REBECCA

Thanks. Are you are going to tell me how you broke your arm?

JOHN

That's an interesting story. It involves impressing my fiancé Jill. As you can see, it didn't exactly turn out the way I intended.

REBECCA

Well, John? Curious minds want to know. Why do men do stupid stuff to impress women?

JOHN

There are two schools of thought on that.

REBECCA

This should be interesting.

JOHN

Trust me, you're going to love it. One school of thought is that it is in our DNA. That's why we do it. No matter how stupid it makes us look. My school of thought, as women like to say about men, quote, "Men are idiots."

REBECCA

That pretty much hits it on the head.

JOHN

Sad part of it is guys will never get the point.

                    REBECCA
Well, at least you can admit it.

                     JOHN
Always been a straight shooter.

                    REBECCA
So what needs to be done around here?

                     JOHN
I need to go to town to pick up some stuff for the wedding.

                    REBECCA
We'll both go to town.

They leave the bed-and-breakfast and head off into town. There's something about living in the country.

                     JOHN
There's something about living in the country.

He looks up to the clear morning blue sky.

                     JOHN
Life in country at slower pace. Compared to the hustle and
bustle of the big city. I couldn't live in big city. I guess I'm
too much of country boy at heart.

                    REBECCA
I suppose in your previous life you were a cowboy riding the
range. Always riding to the rescue of beautiful women being
held by outlaws and bandits.

JOHN

That doesn't sound like too much of a bad life. Sleeping under the stars at night.

A short time later they arrive in town. They park the vehicle. Rebecca gets out of driver's side and walks over to the passenger's side to open the door for John.

JOHN

I thought it was always that it was expected for the guy to open the door for a woman.

REBECCA

Well, what can I say? I guess I'm just too nice.

JOHN

That you are.

At the Farmer's Market, there are people standing at the different fresh produce stands, where fresh produce like apples, oranges, also hand-wooden crafts, are being sold by the local farmers in the area and local craft makers as well.

Rebecca sees a man sitting at the bench with a book in his hands. He is sitting on a bench reading a play by Shakespeare called "A Midsummer Night's Dream."

While John is looking through the fresh produce to bring back to the bed-and-breakfast, Rebecca walks over to him.

REBECCA

Bakery Owner Keith, do you remember me?

BAKERY OWNER

Why, yes.

REBECCA

Sorry to hear about the passing of your wife. I tried to make it to the wake and funeral.

BAKERY OWNER
Rebecca, that's perfectly understandable. You were busy with your career. Being a lawyer in Minneapolis would definitely keep you busy and occupied.

REBECCA
There are times that I do miss my old town. I was so eager to get out of this town, make a life of my own and be independent.

BAKERY OWNER
You were always a very independent person, even while you were growing up.

REBECCA
I inherited it from my mother.

BAKERY OWNER
Probably where you got your thickheadedness as well.

REBECCA
My thickheadedness got me into trouble with my mother while growing up.

BAKERY OWNER
None of us were saints while growing up, except for me.

REBECCA
You're so full of it.

BAKERY OWNER
I won't deny it. Rebecca, what brings you here?

REBECCA

I needed a break from work and since he broke his arm. I still see you have the passion for reading Shakespeare plays.

BAKERY OWNER KEITH

This was one of my late wife's favorite Shakespeare plays, "A Midsummer Night's Dream." There was a quote from the play that she read on our wedding day. I'll never forget. "A proper man, as one shall see in a summer day. A most lovely gentleman like."

REBECCA

No truer words have been spoken.

BAKERY OWNER

So, Rebecca, have you met anybody else since you and John went your separate ways?

REBECCA

Not really. But it hasn't stopped my girlfriends From setting me up on blind dates or them trying to find somebody for me.

BAKERY OWNER

Love finds a way. It may never take a straight path, but it usually finds a way on its own time.

REBECCA

That's very true.

John comes walking over to them.

JOHN

I see that you are both catching up with each other.

BAKERY OWNER

But unfortunately, age caught up with me.

They laugh for a couple of minutes.

REBECCA

I see you still have a sense of humor, like you've always had.

BAKERY OWNER

Well, I'm going to head to the bakery. It was nice catching up with you, Rebecca.

REBECCA

Same with you. Since I'm in town here, I should do some shopping. John, would you like to join me?

JOHN

Do I have a choice?

REBECCA

Not really. Unless you want to walk back to the bed-and-breakfast?

JOHN

Not really.

As they walk down the sidewalk, she sees the town has kept its charm about it. She sees a restaurant is getting ready for its grand opening, also sees a dress shop has opened.

REBECCA

When did that dress shop open?

JOHN

It opened a couple of months ago. The owner of the dress shop sells locally made dresses, plus men's and women's fedora hats.

REBECCA

Let's stop in for a couple of minutes.

The dress store owner greets them as they walk into her store.

STORE OWNER

So how can I help you today?

REBECCA

Well, I haven't bought a new dress for the last couple of years. Also I'd like to take a look at your women's fedora hats as well.

STORE OWNER

What kind of dress are you looking for?

REBECCA

I need a dress that I look damn good in, and also a fedora hat that would go along with the dress as well.

John and Rebecca head back to the bed-and-breakfast.

SETTING: John and Rebecca go down to the Minnesota River.

JOHN

Rebecca, you certainly didn't forget how to skip rocks across the creek?

REBECCA

Of course not.

JOHN

Let's have a bet, shall we? Who can skip at least one rock out of three the farthest across the water? The loser has to take the winner out for supper.

REBECCA

I shall take your bet.

JOHN

Then let the game begin. Ladies first.

REBECCA

Well, how nice of you.

JOHN

Rebecca, have you ever thought about what our life could have been if we stayed together?

REBECCA

John, we wanted different things in life.

JOHN

But we could have made it work between us, right?

REBECCA

John, that was the past. It's best to leave it in the past, all right?

JOHN

You're right.

They start to skip the rocks across the creek to see who will win the bet.

REBECCA

John, if you don't mind me asking, how did you meet your fiancé Jill you are currently engaged to, set to be married to?

JOHN

I was at a friend's engagement party. I was at the bar waiting to get a drink from the bartender. She walked up to the bar. We started talking. Shortly afterward we went out on a couple of dates. Eventually got serious.

REBECCA

She probably couldn't resist your natural charm and wit.

JOHN

I won't. deny that.

REBECCA

So far I have skipped my two small rocks the farthest.

JOHN

This will determine the outcome of the bet.

John throws his last small rock, but it fails to beat the distance of the rock throw by Rebecca.

JOHN

Well, a bet is a bet. Since I lost the bet, I'm duty bound to keep my word.

SETTING: Early evening

Rebecca is standing in front of the oval freefalling mirror in her wine red dress and making up her hair. John knocks on Rebecca's door. Rebecca hears the knocking and turns her head to the guestroom door.

                    REBECCA
        Be there in a couple of minutes.

Then she turns her head back to the mirror.

                    REBECCA
        As my coworker Karen would say, "Damn, girl, you are kill-
        ing it in that dress."

She grabs her wool red fedora hat with a black bow, then walks over to the guestroom door and slides it open and closes it.

                    JOHN
        You look beautiful in that dress.

                    REBECCA
        Thanks. I figured I would wear it tonight. You don't look bad
        in that tuxedo, either.

                    JOHN
        Thanks. What can I say? I wear it well. If you are taking a
        woman out for a night on the town, do it right, I always say.
        So where would you like to go to supper tonight?

                    REBECCA
        I want to try that new Italian restaurant that opened in town
        here that you told me about.

JOHN

Sure, but I need to stop at the stone barn first to let the band know where to reach me in case they need something.

REBECCA

That's all right with me.

They head for the stone barn.

REBECCA

John, this is very impressive. You definitely have an eye for design, that's for sure. What type of wood do you use for the dance floor?

JOHN

I used New England Pine.

REBECCA

Where did you get the idea for the glass dome to be in the middle of the barn roof?

JOHN

I wanted the barn to have a look that caught your eye. So I decided to put in a sky dome in the middle of the roof. I guess you can say I'm just creative.

REBECCA

I never knew you had an interest in architecture.

JOHN

Well, it's just a hobby of mine. Nothing more.

REBECCA

That's not a bad hobby to have.

JOHN

Rebecca, On the night of our high school prom I came down with that nasty bug and was unable to take you. I still owe you a dance. So will you please have this dance with me?

REBECCA

Well, if you insist.

As they start to dance, the band on stage notices them.

BAND LEADER

Sorry to interrupt here, but you can't dance without the proper music.

REBECCA

Well, they are right. So, John, should we dance to a fast song or a slow song?

JOHN

What does the band think?

BAND LEADER

I think this calls for a slow song.

As they start to dance. Rebecca put's her head on John's shoulder. Rebecca and John eye's locked. As if two last lover's being reunited by fate.

JILL

John, what the hell?

JOHN

Jill, you are probably wondering why I'm dancing with my ex-girlfriend Rebecca.

JILL

What would make you say that?

REBECCA

Well, John needed same practice for you guys' wedding dance song. I can't let him make fool of himself. Isn't that right?

JOHN

Never doubt the Rebecca. Plus I wanted to make sure I could still bust a move on the dance floor without busting a kneecap at the same time.

John runs after her and stops Jill at downstage right center, halfway from the barn.

JILL

John, you told me that you were completely over your ex-girlfriend Rebecca.

JOHN

I am.

JILL

It sure the hell didn't look like that way when I walked in on you two.

JOHN

The reason why she is here is she is just staying at the bed-and-breakfast. That's all it is and nothing more.

Rebecca comes walking up behind her.

REBECCA

He is telling the truth.

JILL

All right then. I apologize for being upset back there.

REBECCA

Don't worry about it. I probably would have reacted the same way.

JOHN

So is everything cool and good now?

JILL

Yes. How long have you been a lawyer?

REBECCA

How did you know I was one?

JILL

Because John told me that's what you went to college for.

The next day, while John is standing over the grill cooking the barbecued ribs, Rebecca is setting the picnic table. Jill comes walking over to Rebecca at the picnic table.

JILL

Rebecca, I see how you look at him. Very much like somebody who is still in love with somebody.

REBECCA

That's completely nonsense. I'm completely over him.

JILL

You can fool yourself, lie to yourself. Deny it all you want. You are still in love with him.

REBECCA

Jill, if you are implying that, I'm somehow jealous, because he is marrying you.

JILL

We both want him to be happy.

REBECCA

Of course I want John to be happy.

John comes walking over to them.

JOHN

The barbecued ribs are almost done and about ready.

JILL

I'll be right there.

REBECCA

I'll be there in a couple of minutes.

Rebecca ducks around the corner and sheds some tears. For the first time she faces the decision whether or not to tell John she is still in love with him.

Day of the Wedding

The floweriest and caterer arrive at the bed-and-breakfast for John's wedding to his fiancé, Jill. The family and other guests start to arrive as well.

SETTING: Rebecca enters stage right, walks in to John's room. He is standing in front of the dresser mirror in his wedding tuxedo.

JOHN

Came to help calm my pre-wedding jitters?

REBECCA

I'll be leaving.

JOHN

You're not going to attend the wedding?

REBECCA

I have to get back to my job in Minneapolis.

JOHN

Rebecca, I haven't stopped thinking about that kiss we had in the barn at the end of the song.

REBECCA

John, we were caught up in the moment and nothing more. You are marrying your fiancé' Jill today. Just chalk it up to wedding jitters.

JOHN

You always know me better than I know myself.

Rebecca sheds some tears. John notices Rebecca crying.

JOHN

Rebecca, is everything all right?

REBECCA

I have to go, and congratulations.

Rebecca leave's John room. Head's back to her guest room. She can bear to seeing John. Who she is still in love with. Marrying other woman.

Rebecca is in her room packing her suitcases. Once she is done, she starts to write a note. Before leaving her room, she leaves a handwritten note for John. She then heads back to Minneapolis.

SCENE: Wedding Ceremony

                              PRIEST
John, do you take Jill to be your faithful and loving wife,
until death do you part?

                              JOHN
I'm really sorry about this.

                              JILL
I understand.

                              JOHN
Thank you.

SETTING: *John goes to tell Rebecca she was always the one for him, but it is too late. He sees the note that Rebecca wrote for him.*

John picks up the note that is sitting on the dresser, then sits down on the bed and starts to read it.

Rebecca is standing on the stage, same distance from John, while he is looking at the letter. Rebecca is reading the letter in her own voice.

REBECCA
"Dear John:

I know this isn't proper way. Too tell you good bye. I want you too know. The time we had together. I will never forget. I will alway's cherish. I wish you & Jill. A life full of joy and happiness.

Good bye my Prince. We will alway's be to gether. In my heart. All my days and night's. You will always be in my heart."

John drops the letter and wipes away his tears, then goes back to where Jill is.

JOHN
I guess I am still in love with Rebecca. Those feelings were always there.

JILL
John, sometimes you never get over your first love.

JOHN
Jill, someday you'll meet the right man.

JILL
You'll be a tough act to follow.

Jill leaves the bed-and-breakfast. Bakery Owner and John sit down at a table.

BAKERY OWNER

You look like you have rediscovered something but have lost it again. May never have it again. When Rebecca arrived back in town for a couple of days. you acted differently the whole time she was here. You said once if you never got a second chance with her....

JOHN

But we both agreed to go our separate ways. I didn't want to stand in her way. I could not have asked her to sacrifice that for me.

BAKERY OWNER

John, you never got over her. She was your true love. You were always meant to be with her.

JOHN

That was then and this is now. I can't live in the past.

BAKERY OWNER

If you didn't still love Rebecca, then why did you call off the wedding to Jill?

JOHN

Maybe you're right.

BAKERY OWNER

You could say perhaps I'm an old sentimental fool and old-fashioned. But if I had a second opportunity to be with my true love, even if it was for a single day, I wouldn't pass it up. As that old saying goes, it's better to have love than not to have love at all. Then of course again, I'm just an old man giving advice to somebody who already knows what to do. Sometimes the path we take in life is just a road that leads to the right path to take in life and love.

JOHN

Anybody tell you you are wise beyond your years?

BAKERY OWNER

Yes. You only get wisdom in life if you choose to listen to it.

JOHN

Thank you for the talk and the advice.

BAKERY OWNER

No problem.

SETTING: In the living room of the bed-and-breakfast.

John sits down in a chair and looks at a picture of Rebecca that was taken the night she left for law school. He thinks back to the time they were high school sweethearts. Later the same evening in Minneapolis...

SETTING: Rebecca's Apartment

Rebecca sits down in the window seat bed. Looking up wards to clear blue starry night sky. At the same time shedding tears. Holding an picture of her & John. That was taken at their high school home coming dance. The picture has written on it.

"My beautiful Angel. Who's beauty that out shines. All the star's in the heavenly night sky.

Next day

Karen stops by Rebecca's apartment. Karen knocks on Rebecca's apartment door. Rebecca answers the door and lets Karen into the apartment.

KAREN
So how was your trip to your hometown of Mankato?

REBECCA
Karen, have you ever made a decision earlier in life that you wish you could go back and change?

KAREN
This is about John.

REBECCA
Yes, I thought I would be over him.

KAREN
You still have feelings for him?

REBECCA

Going back to my hometown of Mankato, spending time with him again, just reminded me why I fell in love with him in the first place. He could make me laugh even when I was having a bad day. It also reminded me not to let my second chance to be with him again slip through my fingers.

KAREN

Rebecca, I remember a quote by Shakespeare about love: "Time is very slow for those who wait, Very fast for those who are scared, Very long for those who lament, Very long short for those who celebrate, But for those who have love, time is eternal."

REBECCA

Shakespeare was a wise man.

KAREN

If you ask me, that's some sound advice to follow.

REBECCA

Karen, I don't think any of Shakespeare's words will be able to heal my broken heart.

KAREN

I just remembered, there's something I need to do. I will give you a call later.

John is outside helping some guests when Karen arrives at the bed-and-breakfast.

KAREN

Are you John?

JOHN

Yes, who are you?

KAREN

I'm a coworker of Rebecca's.

JOHN

What brings you here?

KAREN

It's about Rebecca.

JOHN

What about her?

KAREN

Rebecca still loves you.

JOHN

It's too late now.

KAREN

I don't think it is. Sometimes you have to take a leap of faith. I have an idea.

She gets out her cell phone from her purse and calls Rebecca.

REBECCA

What is it?

KAREN

Rebecca, you are to meet somebody by the Florentine fountain statue in Lyndale Park Rose Garden at exactly seven o'clock this evening. It's important.

REBECCA

I'm not exactly feeling like going out.

KAREN

Do it for a friend. One more thing, wear something nice.

Early Evening

Rebecca walks out of her apartment building wearing her wine red dress. She sees a white candle high light horse-drawn carriage with red seats. In the middle of the red seats is a Florazone band of red roses. The driver walks toward her.

DRIVER
Excuse me, miss. Are you Rebecca?

REBECCA
Why, yes, why do you ask?

DRIVER
I will be taking you to Lyndale Rose Garden.

The driver helps Rebecca get into the carriage and then heads for the park. Rebecca notices a card that is between the red roses. She grabs the card and opens it.

REBECCA
"A red rose for a woman who is as beautiful as a red rose is
in the morning as the sun comes up in the morning sky."

They arrive at Lyndale Park Rose Garden at 7:00 P.M. She sees John standing at the Florentine Fountain statue. She gets out of the carriage and walks over to John.

REBECCA
John, what are you doing here? Aren't you supposed to be
getting married?

JOHN

Rebecca, the right woman who I was meant to be with was standing right in front me the whole time. I was a fool not to see it back then.

REBECCA

I guess sometimes fate has a way of working things out. So what's the next step? We leave it up to fate?

JOHN

Well, I would say probably. Not in this case.

They lean in to kiss.